Coffee

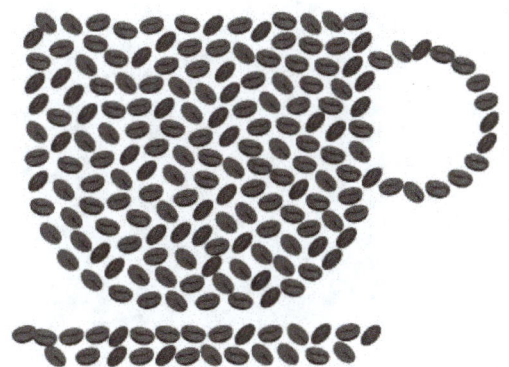

Taonesesa Tiwanna Karidza

A Feature of Club Readership

www.clubreadership.co.za

publishing@clubreadership.co.za

CR Publishers

Publisher

Club Readership

CR Publishers

www.clubreadership.co.za

publishing@clubreadership.co.za

Printed by CR Digital Printers

ISBN

978-0-620-90445-2

This chapbook is crafted with love.

A diligent collection of flowery, nutty, spicy, and smoky prose and poems, written with a pure intention to cultivate a love for books worth a cup of Coffee.

As you read, may you be tenderized into believing you are worth writing a book for because you are!

Here's 'Coffee.'

"Hi Tiwanna,

Thanks for sharing 'Coffee.' I enjoyed reading it, and it was a lovely break from the serious stuff I always read about Coffee. Since my profession is deeply involved in many facets of production, most of what I read is technical. So, I appreciate this change of pace.

Coffee is multifaceted, and it tends to represent the moment in which the beverage is consumed in popular culture. These moments can be both mundane and transformative, each sip like a small 'Pause' button for life - and during busier times can be the only mental respite we get for an entire day. Sometimes it's purely functional, the fuel we need to get through a day's work. At other times it can be the opposite, a good distraction from what needs to be done.

These moments can be simultaneously fleeting and infinite, and most coffee drinkers have more than an appreciation for it. For some, it can be an obsession, a hobby; for others, it's a necessity, and for others, it is a pure pleasure—the aroma and flavour is bliss!

Much has been written about Coffee; this work by Taonesesa Tiwanna Karidza, however, is a unique-yet-familiar collection of thoughts about Coffee, and is a bit like Coffee itself - fleeting, momentary, like a deep breath while looking through a window, the aroma of Coffee wafting around the room. Although they come from the writer's perspective, these phrases, sentences, one-line poems span the moods of many coffee moments - profound and mundane, light and humorous, philosophical, at times a small reprimand and reminder to appreciate something or someone, and always easy to sip and savour.

Suddenly, the book is over, the cup is empty - faint aroma and imperfect memories are all that remains. Luckily for us, there's usually a second read and a second cup if we're willing to take the time and do the work."
- Will Frith

Will Frith was born in Pine Bluff, Arkansas, to a Vietnamese mom and American dad, raised in Texas City, Texas. Before *Coffee*, he worked in a variety of jobs, from retail to construction to foodservice.

He has worked in specialty coffee for 15years, doing all kinds of jobs and leaving each of them on excellent terms.

His *Coffee* career has taken him all over the globe:

Galveston, TX; Olympia, WA; Portland, OR; Singapore; Dalat and Ho Chi Minh City (Saigon), Vietnam. He is currently in Vietnam, running a roasting spot called building.

He's also involved in many projects in the city

(roasting, consulting, education, organizing).

Company: building coffee

Instagram - @building.coffee

"Tiwanna sees the magic in seemingly trivial things. The alchemy of love she expresses through her words is so potent, and it is sensually stimulating. With a delicate balance of mocking humour and a gracious gift of light, she will make love to your mind. "- ShalSdo

Poet

Writer

Storyteller

"I have always called her Taonesesa, because true to her name's meaning, she sees beyond the obvious. As I read Coffee, it feels she is speaking to my soul. The attitude in words is a 'kick' of caffeine. Pun intended.

As the melanin goddess that I am, 'She was a dark roast coffee bean, deep and flavoured...' appealed to me and stroked my ego.

Each person will find themselves in the paragraphs and prose of these odes. Choose to be enriched. Choose to be warmed up from within. Indulge!"-Chiko Chipunza

Accountant

Tax Practitioner

Senior Partner and Founder of GAA Associates.

Founder of MightyWomanProductions - Arts Promotions

She is an African Goddess who is passionate about women, culture, and all things ethnic.

Based in Harare, Zimbabwe.

"As I read the book 'Coffee,' I fell in love with the layout. It reminded me of how customers love to come and dine at Coffee Shops to create a bond, and also, the book touches much on feelings because a Coffee cup can bring love with it. A good Coffee cup is always a great start to my day. I just realized that there's much more to Coffee within the cup.

When Taonesesa told me how much she loves Coffee, reading, and writing, I knew she would be a star.

She has all the qualities of a high-flying glamorous poet. She embodied the coffee story with loving and charming lines, class, and charisma, making you feel the experience of having Coffee with the loved one or friend.

This book is all about appreciating the love of Coffee and understanding its concept and people's perception of Coffee."-Nqobile Bright Mbambo

SCA certified international Barista from KwaZulu-Natal Umlazi

A BOOK ABOUT COFFEE

By Taonesesa Tiwanna Karidza

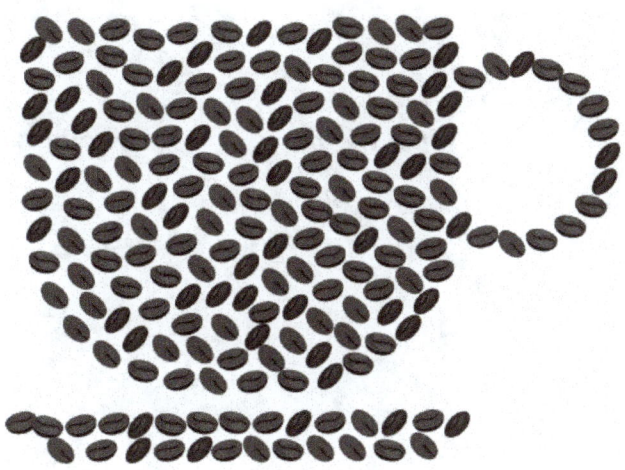

Coffee is a gift from Africa to the World.

You are welcome.

If it's right,
you will drink it all.

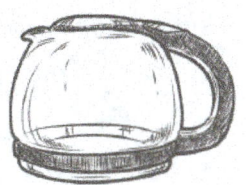

"What's with monks and Coffee?" Asked the monkdrunkwithwine!

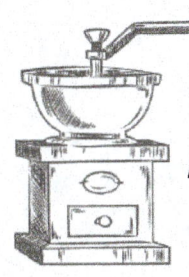

Verbally aromatic,

he richly roasted her with 21 questions.

I was obsessed with the idea of having you like a cup,

but somehow,

you quickly got cold.

She was not Tea.

She was Coffee!

This Coffee has given us a plethora to love again.

Do you crave for me like you desire the intoxication of wine or my floral-y exotic side that leaves you delirious with pleasure?

Then sip me with no milk!

Just like fish, Coffee is great when it is fresh.

When it's stale,

it's abhorrent to the taste buds.

Sometimes the quality of the Coffee

depends on who is drinking it.

When I die,

I will wear my Beautiful Black Birthday Dress

And I will be Drunk,

Caffeinated, woke,

and late to my Burial.

It was written.

After this Coffee,

you will want more.

As you would have it with women,

if the cup of Coffee in your hands is perfect,

it's literally your true love.

The rain came,

and

Coffee was a perfect excuse.

Some prefer their Coffee bean dry,

and natural.

I like my man,

clean and intrinsically flavoured.

Some Coffee dates,

only the cup remembers.

Another bad guy?

Here's a Coffee bean,

on to the next scent.

Freed from his delusions,

the room was not the same.

The Coffee was sadly not the same.

Violence against women had to change!

If I could have Coffee with God,

I would only follow his lead.

Ngicel'ikhofi ?

Sip me slowly,

sip me hot,

sip me cold.

You are a hot coffee on a sunny day,

gracefully cooling my system.

We could have,

but we didn't drink the Coffee.

We drank ourselves until we ran out of sugar!

I hope you taste me in the Coffee.

With the love she put into it,

and her exquisite attention to detail,

the Coffee was underpriced.

She was a dark-roast Coffee bean,

deep and flavoured.

Coffee dates will never be boring if you stop

picking the wrong dates.

We all have different Coffee stories,

what is yours?

After we got high on grass,

drunk on wine, we stayed up in our cups of Coffee

and awaited the sun to rise.

Like the scent of Coffee,

our sexual interaction was as palpable.

"Where do I come from?

How can you drink what you do not know?"

Match the coffee flavours and origin.

Sweet, nutty, spicy

& chocolaty.

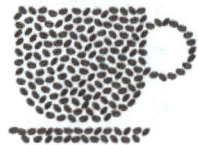

Herby

Acidic, & Fruity.

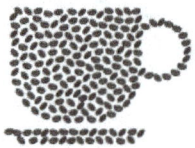

Earthy, & Spicy.

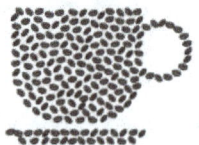

Eu amo café

I would have sipped you quickly,

thank God you are hot!

By desire or by chance we met again,

Coffee or Tea?

I would still do it again.

They said I would stay awake but

I drank it all and I fell asleep.

Whiskey could be great proofing water,

but Coffee is a social lube,

addressing the elephant in the room.

Should I mix you with Chicory

or should I have you straight,

raw and rough?

He is a Coffee house,

and I want all of him!

He was an old classic,

bedazzled in uniqueness.

Like good Coffee, always pleasant.

He was a Coffee lover

and she was like a Coffee stain,

tasteless,

old and unwanted.

He was not Tea,

He was Coffee!

My espresso is perfect for Instagram...

You are a late-day leche,

bad for the tummy.

She was a Turkish Coffee in the hands

of a delighted Turkish man.

You can have me with ice,

extremely hot

or

extremely hot with ice.

You can serve me with salt,

Sugar or

butter.

So long you serve and sip me.....

Take me to cute corner cafes,

buy me Café au Lait and let's talk love,

sex,

Kids and marriage.

She couldn't pick or choose so she became

Yuanyang.

Let's have shots of Coffee and live young forever!

It wasn't the Coffee,

but him who tasted differently.

I will race from Harare to Johannesburg just to sip from the same cup of Coffee with you.

He was eloquent but tasted like old Coffee to me.

He paid for Coffee in exchange he got her heart.

Even if mugs contain hugs,

I would rather drink my Coffee than be with you.

Lost count of the cups!

If only we could see that Coffee fart.

If,

it's what it means to be insensitive,

his Coffee ran out.

She could weigh his pants from the Coffee he drank.

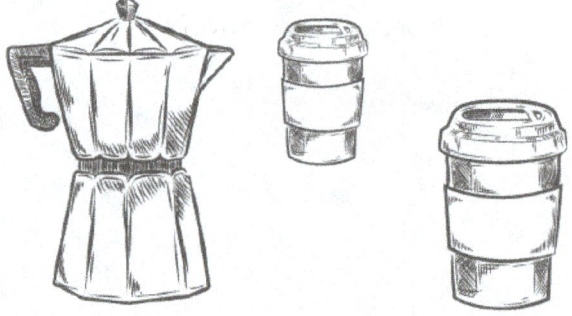

Another cup of Coffee to keep you around ?

It's like she had Coffee bean teeth and a bitter

taste that sent everyone back to sleep.

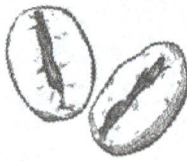

She was a good cup of Coffee!

Each bead on a Catholic Rosary

has its own Coffee flavour.

"Coffee people have to be sexy!"

-Katsu Tanaka

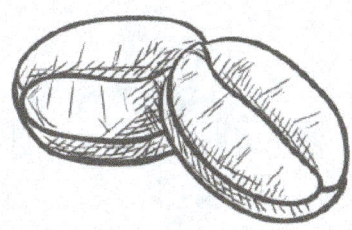

Do not be Coffee that lacks character...

We thank the goat herder for making us a cup of Coffee.

She loved him but,

he didn't like her Coffee.

It's a fruit but you can drink it.

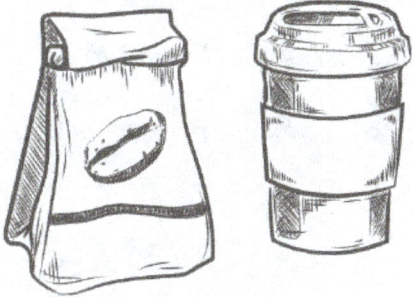

To you,

it could just be Coffee but to the World,

it's the second most traded commodity.

The World's most expensive Coffee comes from poop.

Now that's a lesson for life!

Just as you enjoy Coffee in peace,

enjoy giving people back to the universe.

You could never entirely own them.

Drinking Coffee doesn't mean you are woke!

Let's go Coffee tasting whilst I decide if

I want you or not.....

Every time I try to leave,

the aroma of your Coffee is pulling me back.

It wasn't the Coffee at play that day;

for Coffee had its limits- even her heart

was wide awake.

I thank God for Coffee!

Sometimes it's not the Coffee,

it's the room.

It wasn't Coffee; it was something else

not that good at imitating greatness!

Will you marry me after this Coffee ?

Just after three weeks of knowing him,

like a bad roasted Coffee bean,

he started to be bitter

and he just lost that flavour…

The process of brewing the Coffee

is as important as making the cup.

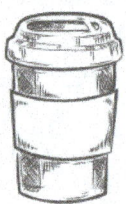

We will only silently say it but finish your Coffee.

Arabica coffee unprepared,

they will surprise you.

Coffee tastes better when you are single

and the barista is hot.

Stand al banco,

the Coffee is cheaper.

Coffee taste better with natural water

but where will we get it?'

Caffe correto just to correct the day!

Be so rich,

you can afford to travel overseas just for the

World's Coffee Roasting Championships!

Every time I try to leave, his aroma pulls me back.

She was into the freshness,

a true enthusiast for Coffee and he was
a stale sip.

She could have been anything else

but she chose to be a moulded Coffee bean,

not worth a cup.

She was a black-eye and the other one

was a light-white, he could not pick or choose.

This is when you take the last sip of Coffee

and we bid Farewell...

Momentarily.

The End

www.ingramcontent.com/pod-product-compliance
Lightning Source LLC
Chambersburg PA
CBHW060335260626
47160CB00007B/2798